Inspirational Scripture & Verse
Susan Blount

 Published by the Peppertree Press, LLC.
the Peppertree Press and associated logos are trademarks of the Peppertree Press, LLC.

For information regarding permissions, write to
the Peppertree Press, LLC.,

Attention: Publisher, 1269 First Street,
Suite 7, Sarasota, Florida 34236

(941) 922-2662
www.peppertreepublishing.com

ISBN: 978-1-934246-11-5
Library of Congress Number: 2006939912
Printed in the U.S.A.
Printed December 2006

This Author's Desire

May the words that I write
Bring the truth to light
May the words from my hand
Give the courage to stand
May the words that I pen
Loose the power within

I believe writing is a reflection of the heart.
As you read each section and reflect on the character of God
it reveals I hope you find your heart responding to Him.

- Susan Blount -

Dear Friends,

*As we walk down this path of life,
at times exuberantly happy and at other
times unbearably sad, may we never
forget that the key to success does not lie
within ourselves, but in the all powerful
hand of The Most High. May we yield to
him our whole lives, and then may he fill
us with his unending love, overflowing
joy, and wonderful grace.*

God Bless You all

*O Lord, God of our fathers,
are you not the God who is in
Heaven? You rule over all the
kingdoms of the nations.
Power and might are in your hand.
And no one can withstand you.
This is what the Lord says to you;
"Do not be afraid or discouraged. . .
for the battle is not yours, but God's.*

*2 Chronicles 20:6-15.
NIV*

Table of Contents

His Might and Glory

His Sacrifice and Love

His Faithfulness and His Care

His Call and His Purpose

His Blessings and His Gifts

HIS MIGHT AND HIS GLORY

THE HAND OF THE MOST HIGH

I know that many times I have clung to an ideal,
Being very certain somehow that I could make it real,
That I could reach this goal and accomplish this great plan.
And every time, I've seen it slip right through my hand,
Leaving me disillusioned, alone, and in despair,
Certain only of my failure, bearing my load of care.
Till my God, in his great mercy, reminded me again,
That absolutely nothing is impossible for him.
For any scheme and any plan
Is nothing till touched by God's hand.
For those things that man cannot fulfill,
By human hand or human will,
Without his touch are incomplete,
But those desires we lay at Jesus' feet
Can be completed, but only by
The mighty hand of the Most High.

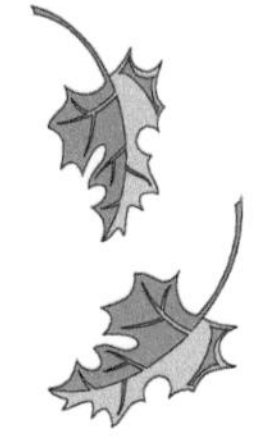

THE MASTER'S CALL

"Come forth," his mighty voice rang out;
All things responding to his shout.
"Yes, come forth, the moon and the sun,
Come forth planets, and stars, each one.
Come forth plants, sky, water and land.
Come forth all creatures, come forth man."

Come to him, Peter, the boat leave,
With faith and courage to believe.
Come forth, the dead man from the tomb,
As the baby breaks forth from the womb.
Come, be filled, all you who hunger,
And be quenched, all you who thirst.

All who are weary and alone,
Come, he will claim you as his own.
Come forth, the broken soul and see
How this one creates life in thee.
For, if you listen and take heed,
You'll find in him all that you need.

"Come forth," – it is the masters call,
"Come forth to me now, one and all."

MY PURPOSE

I am God, and there is no other;
I am God, and there is none like me.
I make known the end from the beginning,
from ancient times, what is still to come.
I say: My purpose will stand, and I will do
all that I please...what I have planned, that
will I do.

Isaiah 46:9-11 NIV

INTERPRETERS

Interpreters may come and go,
But this one thing for sure I know.
The one who made all time and space,
The one who spoke the worlds in place,
Still holds this old world in his hand.
It's still controlled by his command.

Everything he has said, he will do.
What he has destined will come true.
Though evil days may seem so nigh,
Don't let them turn away your eyes.
For we must keep our eyes on him,
If we're to stand until the end.

the WISE

The wise of the world can speculate
all they want.
The spiritualists can meditate
all they want.
But none of that will change
a single thing about who God is.

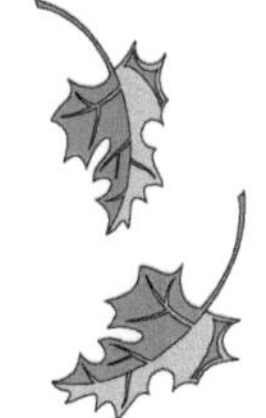

his DISPLAY

He controls all things.
Every fish in every sea
And every bird that sings
Are his entirely.

All the wind that blows
And all the rains that fall,
Every blade of grass that grows
He controls them all.

Yes, and every passing day,
Every beautiful spring flower
Is in his display
They're all within his power.

Be awed by his majesty

I WONDER...

Sometimes when I stand
And feel the cool breeze passing by,
Or sit upon the golden sand,
Or look up at the clear blue sky,

I wonder at God's power so great
That he would a world like this create.
And when the spring is in the air
And the sun so bright shines down,

The joy of love is everywhere
And happiness is all around.
I wonder at God's love so fine,
That he gave me this joy as mine.

Rejoice in his love

THE ALMIGHTY

It takes just a few minutes
Beneath the glory of his sky
To chase away my worries
And bid my doubts goodbye.

The language that it speaks
Is one my heart can hear.
It tells of my Father's greatness.
It says: "There's no need to fear;

For, if he put in place
Every star that's in the night,
There's no problem too big for him,
No battle he cannot fight."

And it takes just a few moments,
Looking with my heart's eye
Upon the cross of Calvary,
Watching my Savior die,

To know this love won't leave me;
I will never be alone.
The Almighty is my Father;
He has called me as his own.

THEIR VOICE

The heavens declare the glory of God; the skies proclaim the work of his hands. Day after day they pour forth speech...their voice goes out into all the earth, their words to the ends of the world.

Psalms 19:1-4 NIV

MY GOD'S MAJESTY

When I behold the heavens you've made, I cannot conceive
Their height and depth; their length and width my mind cannot believe.
But God, what I find harder yet to understand is this,
That you, the God who made each thing that ever was or is.

In this tiny corner of the endless worlds you've molded,
You've chosen the mystery of God to be unfolded,
To battle here your greatest foe; here he'll be defeated
To reveal your greatest work. your masterpiece completed.

That you, the Master of all, would leave your throne in heaven,
And choose to become a man, this humble earth to dwell in;
Would choose to be born, to live, to die the humblest of men...
To suffer shame, rebuke and pain, to die and rise again.

How I marvel when I consider my God's majesty.
But I marvel most to think he would do all that for me.

MINDFUL

When I consider... the work of your fingers, the moon and the stars, which you have set in place, what is man that you are mindful of him, the son of man that you care for him?

Psalms 8:3,4 NIV

THE BLIND

Some foolish men may ask where God is.
Just look around – the world is his.
I see him in the grass and trees.
I feel him in the sun and breeze.
As for those who doubt his presence,
God gave you sight and smell and sense.
He gave you eyes to behold
the beauties of this world untold.
He gave you ears so you can hear
the robin sing and know he's there.
Those who lock God outside their minds –
Those are the ones who are blind
To God's presence and his love.
They won't believe in God above.

MY GOD is an ARTIST

My God is an artist, that no one can deny.
He paints a pretty sunset, or a rainbow in the sky.
He molds the mighty rivers and forms the mountain peaks.
And of his might and power, everything in nature speaks.
My God is an artist, my heart does often cry, when I marvel
At the beauty of his world passing by.

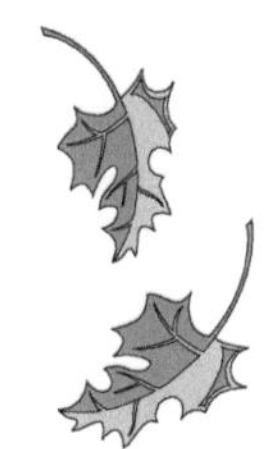

GREAT GOD

For the Lord is the great God, the great King above all gods. In his hand are the depths of the earth, and the mountain peaks belong to him. The sea is his for he made it, and his hands formed the dry land. Come, let us bow down in worship, let us kneel before the Lord our maker.

Psalm 95:3-5 NIV

HIS SACRIFICE AND HIS LOVE

GOD'S LOVE

How great is God's love,

That he, the creator of every living thing, would come and live among them. And...he, the most high of kings, would walk as a peasant! And he, the ruler of all destiny, would die upon a cross!

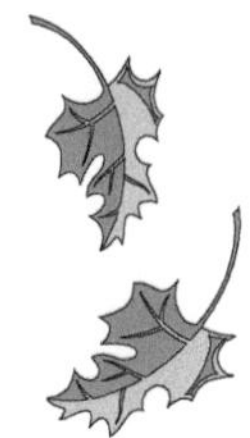

FOR THOSE I LOVE

I wish for those I love the very best. This often isn't prosperity or possessions, but people and the relationships we have with them. I know the most important relationships to me are with my family members. The only relationship more important is my relationship with Jesus Christ. My wish for each of you is to know him. For I honestly believe there is no way to have the best in this life or any part in eternal life without having a personal relationship with him.

How does that happen? It comes from knowing that nothing we could ever say or do could be enough to impress God or buy eternal life, then coming with the eye of our mind to the cross and finding him there, barely recognizable, his face bruised and swollen where soldiers hit him with their fists, blood flowing down his face from the thorny crown he wears. (They made it for the king.) The flesh hangs loose on his back from a roman whip made of leather straps with pieces of glass or metal. his body hangs from a cross, the spikes driven all the way through his hands and feet.

How can this be God? He spoke and created the very universe. He can still speak; then why doesn't he? Surely the voice that created the universe could speak and eliminate those who torture him, but this is what he came to do. For this alone can rescue me from the result of my own rebellion and sin. Only this can make me his. I can not walk away from this kind of love. Instead I will embrace it. How about you?

HE'S EVERYTHING TO ME

Came down from his throne,
Walked this earth alone.
Guess I never knew what love could really mean.
Took my sins away,
Turned my night to day.
Now loving him is everything to me.
Reached down from above,
Filled me with his love.
Guess I never knew what love could really mean.
Touched my very soul,
Cleansed and made me whole.
Now loving him is everything to me.
And on that rugged tree,
He gave his life for me.
Guess I never knew what love could really mean.
Claimed me as his own,
I'll never walk alone.
Cause loving him is everything to me.

He's everything to me, my hopes, my destiny;
my life eternally is his.

HE BORE OUR SINS

He committed no sin, and no deceit was found in his mouth, when they hurled their insults at him, he did not retaliate; When he suffered he made no threats....he himself bore our sins in his own body on the tree, so that we might die to sin and live for righteousness. By his wounds you have been healed.

1 Peter 2:22-24 NIV

THE SILENCE OF THE KING

Before man, you, God, did stand. How could you silent be?
Yet in your meekness was more power than we could ever see.

When they railed at you and accused you still, you held your tongue.
For you alone knew the work that through you must be done

To complete the Father's plan, perfect in every way;
So before the ones you'd made, silent you stood that day.

Everything inside of you must have wanted to cry out,
"Yes, I am King. I am Lord. Yes, I am God" to shout.

In mockery, on your brow they placed that thorny crown.
As the blood began to flow, you uttered not one sound.

They beat and spat on you, then to Calvary you were led.
And as those nails pierced your hands, no rebuke was said.

If you'd but cried to the Father, freed you could have been.
But with your freedom would have been no freedom from our sin.

So God's love and power were revealed, marvel at this thing.
They could only be complete in the silence of the King.

PEACE WITHIN

Why do you run from love so true,
The one who gave his life for you?
Why do you run from peace within,
Freedom from your guilt and sin?
He could have run that dreadful day,
Fled Calvary's Hill and ran away.
He could have run, I know he could,
But instead alone he stood
On Calvary's Hill, my debt to pay.
I'm glad he didn't run away.

Why do you run from God's own Son?

THE TRIAL

Looking back so many years, I find
That dreadful trial on my mind.
An innocent man stood all alone
To pay a debt that was not his own.

"Yes, he's guilty." This they claim;
Blasphemy to God's own name.
Other things they say he's done;
Of these he is guilty of none.
But they sentence him to die,
On Calvary's hill to crucify.

The only chosen Son of God.
"That's fine," You say and turn away.

"Maybe when old I grow,
I'll have no more wild oats to sow.
Then maybe I'll have time to love
This Son of God you tell me of."

Then in my mind I look and see
A trial that is yet to be.
The guilty one stands all alone
To pay the debt that is his own.

What is the charge for sin unpaid?
Then every sin he's done is laid
All there before him to see.
The only answer – a guilty plea.

He looks at the Judge who gave
His only son, that man would be saved.
Oh, if only he could run away,
But now he has his debt to pay.

What horrible agony is in store,
The sentence – hell-forevermore.
The sentence given, the trial through;
I catch a glimpse, could that be you?

And as it is appointed unto men once
To die, but after this the judgment.

God

Hebrews 9:27 KJV

HOW MANY

How many trees are in the forest, how much sand is in the sea
Take each grain and count them that's how much he cares for me
How many stars are in the sky and how long is eternity
For if you can measure these you will know his love for me.

For this reason I bow my knees to the father of our lord Jesus Christ...that you... may be able to comprehend... what is the width and length and depth and height, to know the love of Christ which passes knowledge...

Ephesians 3: 13,18 &19 NKJ

TRUE LIBERTY

To our heritage we cling with honor and with pride.
It was for our liberty that many brave men died.
The price they had to pay they counted not too high.
And by God's grace they managed our liberty to buy.
But like God's chosen people, as the prophets foretold,
When the promised land they claimed, then their hearts grew cold;
They forgot the God who'd taken their bondage away.
Sadly, so it seems to me, it's much the case today.
Our great heritage and honor are something to adore.
But our God that granted them is greater even more.
Sweeter freedom than this he bought, many years ago.
Without freedom that is his, we can't true freedom know.
For though there is no bondage of cruel government,
The bondage and the burden of our sin is greater yet.
So thank him and praise him for the freedom we all claim.
But the soul that gives Christ all, true liberty will gain.
So, let us be humble and submit to God today,
And claim that true liberty that none can take away.

FREE

Then you will know the truth and the truth will set you free...
If the son sets you free you will be free indeed

John 8:32,34 NIV

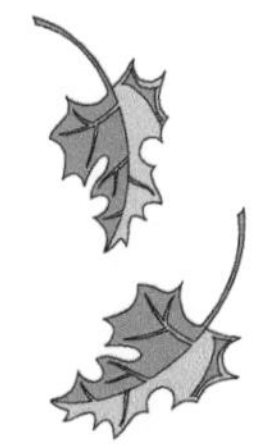

MEANT TO SING THE MASTER'S SONG

If you're a child of God today
And this old world's led you away
From your dear Savior's side to stray,

Please listen closely and hearken to
The words of love I say to you:
"What is this foolish thing you do?

My friend, it makes me very sad
To see that you in rags are clad
When royal clothing you once had.

Where are the treasures, yours to claim
Cause you've believed in Jesus' name?
Of that name are you now ashamed?

And have you left his banquet there
To dine on scraps this world would spare,
When in God's bounty you could share?

Why do you live as peasants would,
When live as royalty you could,
Finding in Christ all that is good?

When was the last time that you thought
What happened when your soul was bought,
The work that God through Christ has wrought?

When have you last looked back to see
Christ hanging there on Calvary,
Bleeding, dying to set you free?

Would you forsake his love so true
And eagerly this world pursue,
After the price he's paid for you?

If he'd but opened heaven's door,
We should desire nothing more
Than to serve him forevermore.

But his blessings there do not end
For us who are the least of men;
Almighty God has called us friend,

Adopted us and made us heirs,
To lift our burdens, know our cares,
And all that's his with us he shares.

What is it that he asks of thee?
Obedience and loyalty,
That Lord of your life he may be.

For to this world you don't belong,
You're meant to sing the Master's song
Come stand with us and sing along.

WALLS

When I thought something had come between my friend and I,
Deep sadness filled my heart and I could not imagine why.
I didn't want walls between myself and those for whom I cared;
Why, some of the sweetest times were when in fellowship we've shared.
How happy and relieved was I when I at last did find
There was no wall. It had all been imagined in my mind.
And as I came before the Lord that very night in prayer,
I thanked him for that fellowship and walls that were not there.
And as I thought of my own sorrow my heart began to cry.
How many times had I built walls between my Lord and I?
I did not want to lose the joy between me and my friend.
Yet so many times I put things between myself and him.
How many times I know I've caused him sorrow and despair,
The times he wanted my fellowship and I was not there.
How could I act so foolishly to treat my God that way?
And yet in spite of all of that, my faithful friend will stay.
And so I come and ask that he forgive me once again,
Tear down my walls and draw me ever nearer to my friend.

ONLY ME

Though he has so many other children just like me,
When I come before his presence with humble heart and bended knee,

He makes it seem that the only one he cares about is me,
And he listens to each meager word, oh so carefully.

It makes me wonder when I think this could really be,
That the mighty God I worship should love someone like me.

And love it is that no one else can love so tenderly.

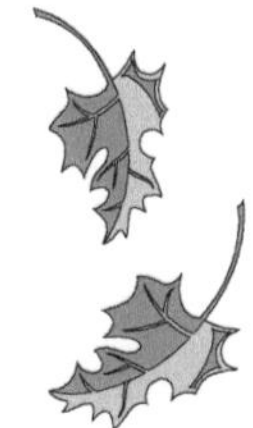

GARBAGE OR GOLD

In each man's heart there's a scale on which he must weigh
The things he will cling to, and the things he will turn away.
On one side, Christ the Savior, in love his life he gave;
The other, sinful pleasure whose end is the grave.
On one the false glitter of this world and it's treasure;
On the other all Christ's riches far beyond measure.

Will you tell me, my friend, as on your balance you weigh?
Which will be your choice, what will your answer be today?

Will you accept my Jesus, or to your sin still hold?
Which one will you cling to – this world's garbage or Christ's Gold.

I have suffered the loss of all things and do count them worthless that I may win Christ...

Philippians 3:8 NKJ

MY FATHER'S HOUSE
(THOUGHTS OF A PRODIGAL)

I remember when my Father's house was a dreary place to be.
It became very plain to see there was nothing there for me.
The world seemed to mock me with its freedom and it's charm,
So I left my Father's house behind and fell into its arms.

At first it seemed to give me everything I hoped to find.
And I very seldom thought of all the things I'd left behind.
But now the rain has stopped and everything is cracked and dried.
The things I once found so attractive have withered and died.

Everyone is gone. I've nothing left. No place to go . . . I am alone.
And my hungry heart's beginning to look toward home.
Now that I recall all the treasures behind my Father's door.
I'm wondering why I ever left the life I had before.

There was always so much bounty, more than enough to share,
Never any want for those whose shelter was his care.
Loving Father, loving master, always caring for his own...
Now I know there are no treasures like those in my Father's home.

The more I think about it, the more I want to see his face.
The more I remember, the more I long for his embrace.
In all the world I know there's nothing that ever could compare
To my Father's house because my Father's always there.

Now I'm running down the road. It won't be long until I see
My home, and the figure I know is waiting there for me.
Once I reach my home and Father, this journey will end.
One thing I know for sure...I will never leave again.

"How great a love the Father has bestowed upon us,
That we should be called children of God. ...
1John 3:1 NIV

LOVED BY THE KING

I saw my King today as he passed by me
and Oh! What a glorious picture to see.
He was so gallant and his image so fine,
and then as he passed by, his eyes met mine.

How could I dare to imagine the thought
That he could love me, for I know he could not.
He could not love me, for he is too grand.
Too great his majesty, too mighty his hand.

There is nothing I could do to draw him to me
For I've no wealth, no beauty, no honor to see.
For I'm just a peasant, a slave girl and I
Will labor in bondage till the day that I die.

So to my labor I return once again,
Knowing surely his favor I could never win.
But as I return, blessed news I am brought.
My price has been paid and my freedom is bought.

But who has paid such a price? Who could it be?
Who would pay such a price for someone like me?
Then as my chains are loosed and freedom is mine,
I look up and to my surprise I find

The King's my Redeemer! My savior is he!
Suddenly I no longer want to be free.
To be near him And serve him will be my life's task.
If he'll just let me serve him, no more will I ask.

As the King draws near, and his hand reaches out,
I know that he loves me, there is no doubt
That his love has sought me and brought me this day
And that his love will never turn me away
Surely my life could never be as it was
For he loves me; he loves me; he does.

Be glad and rejoice with all your heart.
The Lord has taken away your punishment.
He has turned back your enemy.
The Lord, the King of Israel is with you;
The Lord your God is with you,
He is mighty to save. He will take great delight in you.
He will quiet you with his love.
He will rejoice over you with singing.

Zephaniah 3:14-17; NIV

THE DANCE

This world comes with its alluring smile
Saying, "Come with me, lets dance awhile.
I'll dance with you on polished floors,
Meet your desires and even more,
And as I gently hold you close
You'll find the things you want the most."
And in my heart I'm pondering
And in my mind I'm wondering...
About this offer that he makes...
Choosing which step I should take.
Then a strong voice says from behind,
"You must leave – this one is mine."
I turn and find my true love is
Reaching out for what is his.
Now we are dancing face to face,
I'm resting in his strong embrace,
As his arm draws me to his side
And his hand firmly holds to mine.
As I receive his gentle kiss
My stubborn will is lost in his.
Who would not choose a love like this?
A love this strong, who could resist?
So in these arms I choose to stay
Eternally, not just today!

ARM

There is an arm that holds the weakest.
There is a hand that leads the blind.
There is strength found only in meekness.
There is a love I know it's mine.

HIS FAITHFULNESS AND HIS CARE

HIS MIGHTY PRESENCE

IT IS El Elyon, All Mighty One, who holds my hand and leads.
IT IS Jehovah-jireh, my provider, who meets all of my needs.
IT IS Jehovah-shalom, the One who is my Peace;
when he speaks, "Be still," all my raging storms cease.
IT IS Jehovah-rapha who is Physician great,
who can heal all my brokenness and new life create.
IT IS Jehovah-mekoddishkem, he who takes away my sin
and leaves his own righteousness to purify within.
IT IS Jehovah-sabaoth, Lord of the mighty hosts,
who always watches over me and never leaves his post.

This all powerful one is my Provider and Peace.
He is my Physician, Purifier, and Protector.

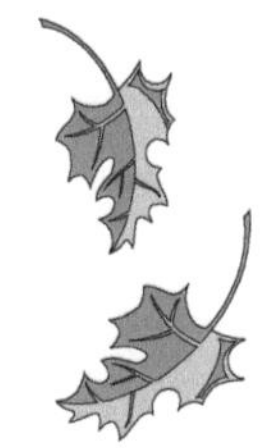

SPEAK OF HIS POWER

If you knew my God the way that I do,
If you knew my God and he knew you,
We would talk for hours and hours on end
And tell all about this special friend.
We'd speak of his power; we'd speak of his might,
We'd speak of him far into the night.
We'd tell of his love, so faithful and true,
Of trials and storms it's carried us through;
That his ever-bountiful hand can impart
Not only our needs but desires of our heart.
For no greater pleasure or joy could we find
Than to speak of our Savior so gentle and kind.

Give thanks to the Lord, call on his name. Make known among the nations what he has done. Sing to him, sing praise to him; tell of all his wonderful acts. . . let the hearts of those who seek the Lord rejoice!

Psalm 105:1-3 NIV

MY FORTRESS

He's my fortress strong and tall!
Safe I hide within his wall.
Master, Ruler, Lord of all.

In his love I will abide.
There I know that I may hide
From the storms that rage outside.

Though this body they may rend
That for now I dwell within,
My soul they can't enter in.

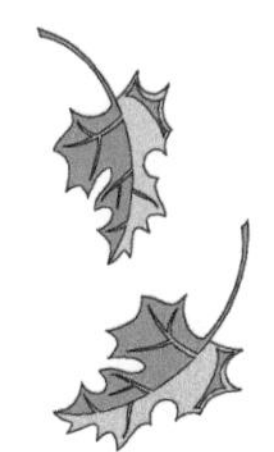

LORD YOU ARE MY SHELTER

Lord, you are my shelter from the world. When I have problems, you're my counselor. When I am troubled, you're my comforter. When I'm in need, you're my provider. When I am in danger, you're my protector. When I am in trouble, you're my defense. When I am weak, you're my strength. All the time, you're my best friend, and all my life you will be my God.

THROUGH IT ALL

Lord, I can't hide from you.
I know you're always there.
Every time I turn from you I know that you still care.
Lord, I can't run far before I turn and find you there.
And you know I'll always love you through it all.
I know at times, Lord, I don't give you all and all;
Times when you call me, and I don't listen to your call,
The times when I slip, Lord, and, yes, the times I fall.
But you know that I still love you through it all.
My Lord, you know my heartbeat and every battle fought.
And you know my deepest and most secret inner thought.
And every time I've run from you
And after me you've sought,
I know that you still love me through it all.

Where can I go from your Spirit? Where can I flee from your presence? If I go up to the heavens, you are there; if I make my bed in the depths, you are there. If I rise on wings of the dawn, if I settle on the far side of the sea, even there your hand will guide me, your right hand will hold me fast.

Psalms 139:7-10 NIV

THE VALLEY

Sometimes my God says, "Through the valley you must go."
And I look up and say, "Why the valley so low?"
His answer comes back to me with his loving care:
"Do not be frightened, for I will go with you there.
I've been through the valley and you must go,too,
If others around are to see me in you.
You see, beyond the valley's a mountain so tall,
And if you're not ready you'll stumble and fall.
Like the metal made into the head of an ax,
My child must be tempered to stand Satan's attacks.
Till it's cut and polished a gem is just a stone.
And thus are my children, till the valley they've known.
I would not send you where you're not able to go
And so my child this is why the valley so low.
Don't be discouraged for great works you will do,
But for right now the valley you have to go through.

...this is what the Lord says – he who created you, ..., he who formed you, ... "Fear not, for I have redeemed you; I have summoned you by name; you are mine. When you pass through the waters, I will be with you; and when you pass through the rivers, they will not sweep over you. . .Since you are precious and honored in my sight, and because I love you..."

Isaiah 43: 1,2,4 NIV

KEEPER OF MY SOUL

Lord, sometimes you find me lonely where everyone has left me all alone.
Then one lone raindrop falls on me, just a reminder that I am your own.
I was thinking that no one could really care.
My God, how could I forget that you were there?
And sometimes when despair finds me, I go and find a quiet place to be.
Then you send the sweet birds melody as you gently wake my fading memory.
How can I dwell on all the things that are wrong
When your great glory surrounds me in that song?
Like the straying sheep, I'm restless; how many times I wander from your side,
Yet every time your faithfulness reminds me that in your love I can hide,
Reminding me that you're the keeper of my soul;
God, I am yours and you are in control.

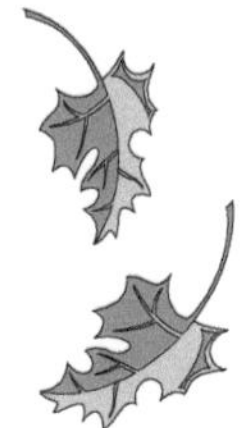

KEEP US, DEAR JESUS

Dear Jesus, our Savior, keep us from harm,
Safe in the shelter of your loving arms.
Keep from the tempests that face us each day,
Keep us, dear Jesus, from wandering away.
Save from the arrows that Satan would hurl.
Keep us unspotted from this sinful world,
Free from our own selfishness and greed,
That we may be pure in word and in deed,
That we may not plant bitterness and strife.
Cleanse us and wash us with your "Words of Life".

YOUR BEST

I deserve nothing but sorrow and pain
But dark clouds and rain.
Still over and over again
You give me the best that you can.

I'll never understand why you love me so-
Some things I will never know.
But because I know you do
I must return my love to you.

Sometimes I know I fail to be
All that you had planned for me.
But through my failures you've still blessed
And always gave to me your best.

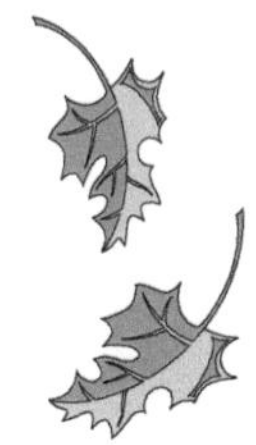

PRAISE

Praise the Lord, I tell myself and never forget the good things he does for me. He forgives all my sins and heals all my diseases, he ransoms me from death and surrounds me with love...he fills my life with good things...he has not punished us for all our sins nor does he deal with us as we deserve. For his unfailing love toward those who fear him is as great as the height of the heavens above the earth.

Psalms 103:2-11 NLT

HAVE YOU NOT HEARD

Tell me my soul why are you cast down?
Don't you remember the truths you have found?
Is not God your refuge, Jesus your might?
Has he not promised your battles to fight?
The precious promises found in his word
Soul, have you not known? Have you not heard?

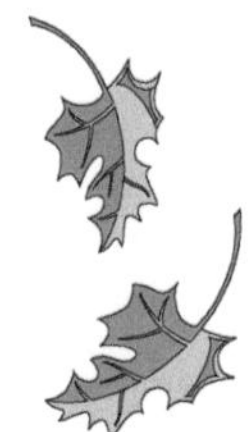

CONFIDENCE

If I am truly confident in Gods power and his love,
can I lift the burden of care, worry or stress?
Can I complain or be discontent? To do so is to confess
his power is not able to take care of this need.
If his power is able then his love must not be enough.
But I know this is not so.

If you...know how to give good gifts to your children, how much more will your Father in heaven give good gifts to those who ask him?

I will not say my Father has given me something bad.
I must hold to his promise that all things will work out for his glory,
my good and the good of others.

CHRIST LOVE

Can anything ever separate us from Christ's love? Does it mean he no longer loves us if we have trouble or calamity, or are persecuted, or are hungry or cold or in danger or threatened with death?... No, despite all these things, overwhelming victory is ours through Christ, who loved us. And I am convinced that nothing can ever separate us from his love. Death can't, and life can't. ...Our fears for today, our worries about tomorrow...nothing in all creation will ever be able to separate us from the love of God that is revealed in Christ Jesus our Lord.

Romans 8:35-39 NLT

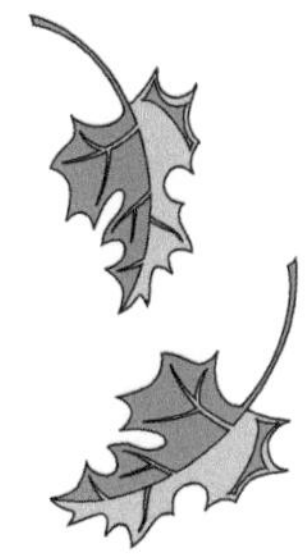

HIS CALL AND HIS PURPOSE

PURPOSE

There is no purpose but in the Lord, no hope, no reasoning, no anything but in the Lord. Men strive only to please themselves and yet in vain for they are not satisfied. Men kill and abuse with no thought of human life or dignity. I can not put my trust in them. Then where can I go but to the Lord? I cannot cling to ashes and that is all the world is ashes. Sorrows, griefs, complaints, hurts. Even the most solid things crumble to nothing.
No one can promise me a tomorrow or what will be in it.
So let me cling to you, oh Lord. Just let me cling to you.

Can you truly find anything else to put your hope in?

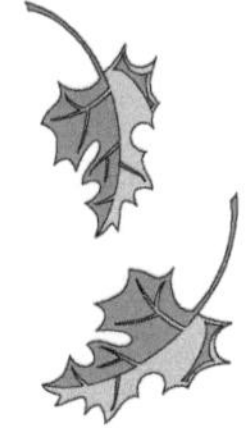

KNOWN

..."Let not the wise man gloat in his wisdom, or the mighty man in his might, or the rich man in his riches. Let them boast in this alone: that they truly know me and understand that I am the Lord who is just and righteous, whose love is unfailing, and that I delight in these things.

God

Jeremiah 9:23&24 NLT

TO KNOW US

To know us, to be known by us, this is his desire. This is what he made us for, what he requires from us.
Relationship
As we know him better we find the faith and confidence to give him control of our lives.
Surrender
When we do this we discover the ultimate truth, when we give up our lives to him, he can and will live through us.
Awesome Power

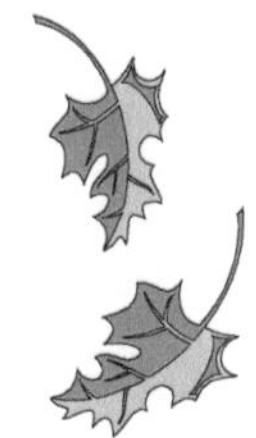

ALL I NEED TO KNOW

Lord, sometimes I wonder what tomorrow will hold.
Trouble, pain and sorrow or riches of silver and gold.

It's not for us to know what tomorrow might bring.
Will it make me cry a tear or will it make me sing?

That's a question the answer I never will know.
But I know my God controls it all, that's all I need to know.

THE GARDEN

As I look back, I see all the seeds I have sown.
If I could have seen the fruit, if I had known
The sorrow and grief they'd bring me someday,
Then surely I wouldn't have planted that way.

For I can see how I planted carelessly
Those things that are now bringing sorrow in me.
For, as in a garden, our lives bring around
The things we have planted in the furrowed ground.

So, my friend, be ever so careful, I pray,
Of those things that you're planting today.
For the things you are planting today, my friend,
Will come back tomorrow, again and again.

Sometimes it's not sowing but having not sown
Those things that tomorrow we want to have grown.
For, if the seed we plant is only one kind,
When the harvest comes that is all we will find,

For those things in the future you want to know,
You must be faithful in the present to sow.
So be careful, faithful, diligent to toil,
Ever placing our seeds in life's fertile soil.

"Do not be deceived: God cannot be mocked.
A man reaps what he sows."

Galatians 6:7 NIV

PLANS

…"For I know the plans I have for you,….plans to prosper you and not to harm you, plans to give you hope and a future. Then you will call upon me and come and pray to me, and I will listen to you. You will seek me and find me when you seek me with all your heart.

God

Jeremiah 29:11-13 NIV

Give me eyes so I can see.
Show me the plans you have for me.
Lead me through that open door.
I long for you and nothing more,
I long for you and nothing more.

THE NET

God will give you a story. he will orchestrate the events of your life weaving them like a net to catch those who are falling and to change the world.

"...I will make you fishers of men." ~Jesus

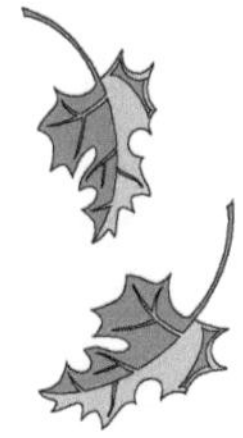

HUMANNESS

We tend to excuse ourselves by saying we are not Jesus.
He was perfect and we are human.
We settle for our humanness and accept it.
But the truth is, although we are human and cannot be Christ,
when we totally surrender to him, he can conquer our humanness.

RIGHTEOUSNESS

How many times do I think I am spiritual when so much of my life is not? How can I settle for mediocre when my God knows nothing of mediocrity, nothing of lukewarmness, only what he finds in my life. The shallowness of what I think of others or what they think of me is not of him. God, I want to know your greatness and not my weakness, that I may experience true spirituality, that of being filled and controlled by your spirit. Lift me above my sinfulness and let me know your power in me; bring me to your true righteousness.

Your Child.

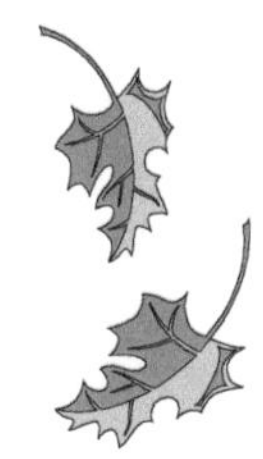

JUST MY MASTER'S SERVANT

I'm just my Master's servant, but a
faithful servant I must be.
My job is to serve, and care for the
things he has trusted to me.
I dare not grasp or claim anything,
for the Master owns it all.
And the power is his to keep, to care for, to make
stand or to let fall.
To lift up, exhort or comfort another servant
my job may be;
But it's the Master's job to see that others
serve him faithfully.
As my Master and Lord, he promises to
meet my every need;
But only as I trust in him will he cause me to
succeed.
So may I find my strength in Jesus, trusting
in his mighty hand,
And in the storms of life find there the
power I need to stand.
For everything I could ever need can be found
in his grace;
Peace, rest, and victory come when I meet God
face to face.

LESSONS

This life is a never-ending line of lessons, each one designed to bring the Christian closer to the image of Christ. Every pilgrim is on his own lesson, just as I am. May I never judge another. Instead, may I rejoice that I am counted worthy of this labor of God's love, and not resist wholeheartedly the work he is doing.

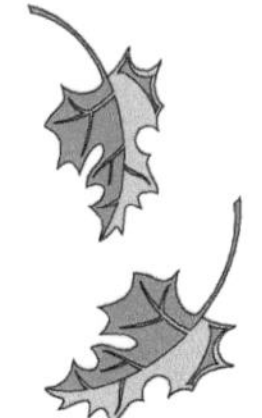

TRIED IN THE FIRE

Tried in the fire, what will it be?
What will it take to empty me?

Of sinful pride and vanity,
And cleanse from all idolatry,
To empty out my treasure chest
Of all those things that I possess,

Or rather those that possess me?
What will it take set me free?

While I offer every vain excuse,
And you must try to pry me loose
From the clutter that I hold so dear
That keeps you Lord from drawing near.

Tried in the fire, what will it be?
What will it take to empty me?

To consume all that I withhold,
Bring forth my soul as purest gold,
Till this greatest treasure I have known,
To be possessed by you alone.

IDOLATRY

Lord,

Am I willing to pay the price of discipleship? Would I give up all for you? I wonder. And then I look at the blessings that balance the scale and I have to say, "Yes!"

Please forgive me Lord. I shouldn't have to see the blessings. My love responding to your love should be enough. Help me to empty my treasure chest of things I hold valuable, giving them to you. And may I hold nothing more valuable than you, my Lord.

Isn't that the bottom line of all my sin? If you were more important than my rights, my pleasure, my comfort, my treasure, then my sin would be gone.

Cleanse me of idolatry.

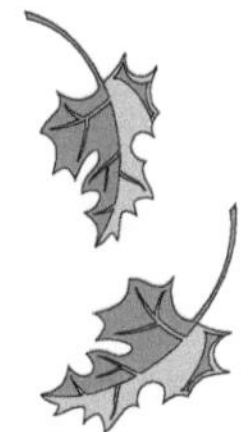

SLIP AWAY

Time is a gift that God has given, a treasure to invest.
Will we spend our days in pleasure or hold onto God's best?
If we waste the time God's given, what is the price we'll pay!
For we can't see the joys ahead or the dreams we'll throw away .
Throw away
Throw away

When all the time slips away and we meet with God some day,
Will he reveal to us what could have been had we chosen to obey?
Don't you think it's time to weigh tomorrow on the scale of today.
And learn to use each moment wisely, before they slip away .

Slip away
Slip away

"Teach us to number our days aright, that we may gain a heart of wisdom."
Psalm 90:12 NIV

HIS WORKMANSHIP

He is the potter, shaper, molder, of our lives. We are the clay to be shaped and molded. The clay must yield to the potter's touch and not resist. Clay already shaped and hardened cannot be molded; it is useless. So we surrender to his touch that we may become his workmanship, his masterpiece. Imagine! He is lovingly, carefully, shaping me into his very own masterpiece. When he is finished, what is it I expect to see? A vase, a jar, even a funnel for him to pour through? All these would be useful I think, but I am amazed when he is done to see that he has shaped me into the very image of himself.

For we are God's workmanship, created in Jesus Christ to do good works, which God prepared in advance for us to do.

Ephesians 2:10 NIV

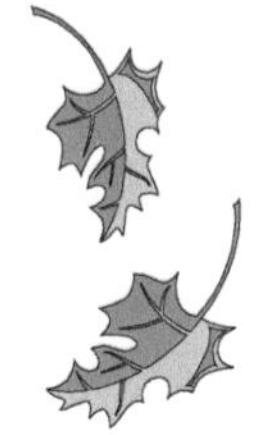

ISN'T ME

Dear God,

You have given us a job to do, but we can't do it. We will share what you give us to share, teach what you give us to teach. But don't let us forget that it isn't us, our wisdom, our love, our friendship, but yours that others need. And it's your job. Thank you for the privilege to be a tool in your hand.

"In a large house there are articles not only of gold and silver, but also of wood and clay; some are for noble purposes and some for ignoble. If a man cleanses himself from the latter, he will be an instrument for noble purposes, made holy, useful to the Master and prepared to do any good work."

2 Timothy 2:20, 21 NIV

MYSELF, MY ENEMY

Father I want to follow you, but all to often fail.
The things I know I should not do, those I do too well.
Myself is a constant enemy of all that is of thee.
Yet when you have it beat and bound, I seek to set it free.
I play a dangerous game with this monster within.
I act as though it's harmless, even treat it as a friend.
Show me its' fangs, its' wrath that seeks to destroy me.
O God, rescue my soul I pray, from self my enemy.
I cannot wield the sword to slay, my strength cannot endure.
I know within thy hand alone the victory is sure.
There is no power greater than thee, no enemy can stand,
Once we realize the secret lies in surrender to thy hand.

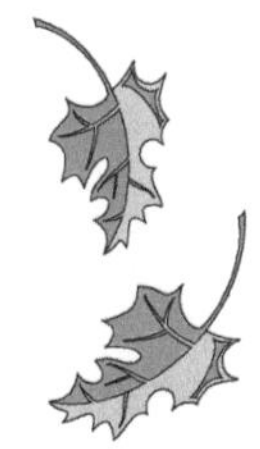

THE WATER OF THE SPIRIT

Like a dam holding back a great wall of water, when it is opened the water gushes out.
It washes away with tremendous force everything in its path.

The waters of God's Spirit are waiting to have the dam of our resistance taken away.
Then the Holy Spirit will flow with incredible power.

He will wash away every obstacle in your life and flood the world around you!

RIVER

Gods power flows like a mighty river. He calls us to find in total abandon the depths of all he is. By faith we are to plunge into its flow and be swept away by it. And yet more often we are content to stand ankle deep and watch the river flow, knowing there is so much more.

TRULY LIVE

To lose this life is to truly live
And to live for self is to die,
To surrender all my life to Christ
And this selfish will to crucify.

To long for this world is to lose him;
To long for him is to lose this.
Which one to gaze into the eyes of,
Which one to embrace and kiss?

Each one calls for our allegiance,
Each calls to be our hearts desire,
But to give our true devotion
Surely does a choice require.

Do not love the world or anything in the world.
If anyone loves the world, the love of the Father is not in him.

For we know that our old self was crucified with him...
that we should no longer be slaves to sin.

1st John 2:15 NIV
Romans 6:6 NIV

BATTLE CRY

Soldier, are you ready for this battle?
Are you ready for this test?
Will you follow your Commander,
Forsaking all the rest?

Will you draw your sword to fight?
Will you raise the battle cry?
For the King and for his kingdom
I will live and I will die.

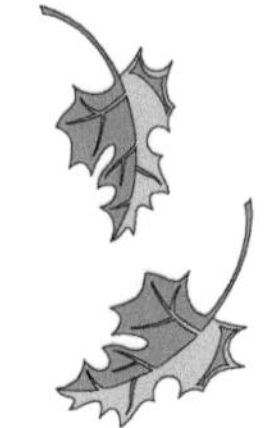

HIS BLESSINGS AND HIS GIFTS

DEAR GOD

Dear God,

Let me keep a written record and reminder of our love for each other. We are best friends. No one is as faithful, kind and understanding as you. Thank you for the wonderful gifts and blessings that fill my life. Thank you for the joy of sharing others' lives, my family and my friends. I pray we will build each other up to be more like you.

Your Friend,

Sue

Certainly, the greatest gift we are given besides life eternal is the gift of others.

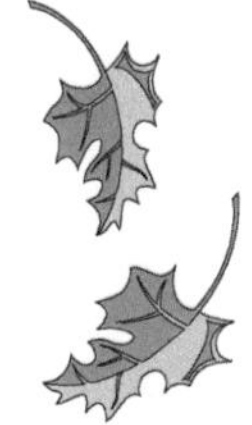

A MEMORIAL TO WILL

On December 21, 1974, I married my dear husband William Blount Jr., better known as Will. He was a big man with a big heart. He loved his children, his family and his friends. He was generous and kind. Helping others was something he loved to do. He adored me, always spoiling me with gifts and compliments.

On February 12, 2006, he passed from this life into one that will never end. His passing has left a hole in many hearts and a stark awareness of the frailty of life. He is missed.

HOW LONG

Our days are numbered and we don't know, young or old,
How long we have for our story to be told.

How long for hugging or laughing with friends,
Till we cross that river and this story ends.

How long for kissing and holding a child close,
And for figuring out what matters the most.

How long for teasing and silly replies,
Till we're left with "never agains" and tearful goodbyes.

There's no more time for hugging and laughing with you;
No more time for doing the things we wanted to do.

Still, you're not truly gone, in our hearts you remain.
With your love and sweet memories till we're together again.

I love you Honey,

Sue

HIS WONDEROUS PRESENCE

What true pleasure can we have below,
Lest we his precious presence know?
All else is vanity.

And no greater joy than this be known,
Than when this mortal soul has flown.
My friend, haste it to flee.

Where no trouble, pain or trial there
In that exquisite place to bear,
Where I his face shall see.

Don't hold to me but bid me go
Where I his wondrous presence know
Throughout eternity.

But make sure your own soul trust in him
As redeemer, savior, master, friend,
And you will join with me.

"Do not let your heart be troubled ...I am going to prepare a place for you...that you also may be where I am ..."

Jesus

HIS CHILD

Of the eight children I have given birth to it is very obvious that some of them bear little resemblance to me. They look very much like their father. Sometimes something they say or do is so much a reflection of him. It is very clear that they are his children. As I walk through this life I should be a mirrored image a reflection of my father. When others look at me I hope they know I am his child.

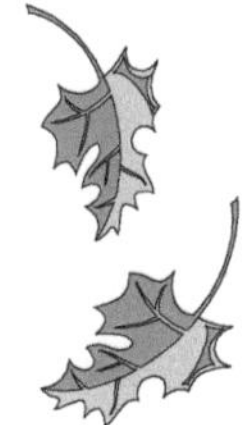

HOW PRECIOUS A GIFT

How precious a gift.
How priceless a treasure;
The worth of this life,
Nobody can measure.
For the things of this world
Will vanish away,
To wither and fade;
Disappearing someday.
But the soul once conceived
Is destined to be
In existence for all eternity.
No greater privilege could anyone ask
No greater privilege, yet no greater task,
Than to nourish and train:
To nurture and raise
A life that can bring to God
Glory and Praise!
Glory and Praise!

"Sons are a heritage from the Lord,
Children a reward from him".

Psalm 127:3 NIV

TEACH US, LORD, TO CHERISH

Today I stopped and opened an old photo book.
I stayed there awhile to linger and to look.
As I did, I looked at each smiling little face,
Each child so full of wonder, so easy to embrace.

Once more I realize how quickly time has passed.
The wonder of today will but for a moment last.
Embraces are fewer, the little boy disappears;
A young man will replace him ~ how quickly pass the years.

The little girl smiling from the ladder on the slide...
Before I know it she could become some young man's bride.
As the preciousness of these lives turns into memory,
And the joys that I know today will no longer be,

Teach us, Lord, to cherish these precious gifts you've given.
Don't let our joy be robbed by the pressures that we live in.
Help us to rejoice with ever-thankful hearts
And embrace every blessing that your great hand imparts.

"Every good and perfect gift is from above."

James 1:17 NIV

SOME DAYS

In the land full of children
where I lived for so long,
There was so much to do, life
moved quickly along.
Some days filled with laughter
but too many were just full,
For there were errands and chores,
and work and school.
Still some days filled with playgrounds
and slides and swinging,
And others with giggles and reading
and singing.
Some days filled with waves and
water and sand,
Some of the days in this children
filled land.
But it's for certain they were far, far
too few,
For there were much too many things to
do.
I turned away for a moment; it
wasn't for long,
And when I looked back, the
children were gone.
Through the land of lost children
I searched everywhere;
I looked and looked but they
were not there.
Finally to the land of grown children
I came.

It was there that I found
them but they were not the same.
So if you find yourself in this
child-land today,
Don't be quick to leave and don't turn
away;
Not for one single moment or
this lesson you will learn.
Once you leave this land you can
never return.

LORD, HUG SOMEONE FOR ME

Lord there's someone dear to me who I can't be
with today.
Someone who I want to see, some things I want to say.
I wish they were here with me. But instead, they're
far away.

So Lord, hug someone for me and remind them that I care.
Tell them how much I love them, and that I wish I
were there.

Help them to remember me, although busy they may be,
Let them send a thought my way, Lord.
Please hug someone for me.

I feel as though we have taken a journey together. You have given me the great privilege of sharing my heart, my thoughts and my God. I hope they have been an encouragement to you. If you do not have a personal relationship with Jesus Christ, I truly hope you will come to him; you will find him waiting with open arms. In conclusion, I offer this last poem as my prayer and I hope yours also.

Your Friend,
Susan Blount

WALK WITH ME, LORD

Walk with me, Lord, down paths I don't know.
Through troubles and blessings, help me to grow.
Sorrows may find me, storm clouds may roll;
Sweet Lord, through it all shelter my soul.

Walk with me, Lord, down paths I don't know.
Help me to others your love to show.
No matter where the long road may lead,
Don't let me forget you're all that I need.

Walk with me, Lord, stay right by my side;
Ever your comfort and love shall abide.
All I can ask, sweet Jesus, my friend
Is to walk with me, Lord, all the way to the end.

www.ingramcontent.com/pod-product-compliance
Ingram Content Group UK Ltd.
Pitfield, Milton Keynes, MK11 3LW, UK
UKHW041851190726
13854UKWH00002B/835